RICE&
BEANS
AND
COLLARD
GREENS

Finding the Vital Ingredients
to a Healthy Marriage

DENISHA SANCHEZ

VIRTUE
PRESS

Homeguides.sfgate.com
(Articles: "When is a Good Time to Plant Collard Greens" and "Can Collard Green Plants take a Frost")

theowlstrust.org
(Article: Understanding Owls)

divorcestatistics.info
(Article: Some Devastating Effects of Divorce in the USA)

Scripture KJV unless otherwise stated.

Printed in the United States of America.

ISBN-13: 978-17353705-0-7

Virtue Press

I dedicate this book to

My children, my greatest gifts, Eliseo Jr and Faith Jessie:
    From the moment God blessed me with you both, it has been my desire to be the best Mother to you. I wanted to do the things for you, I had only imagined were possible. To introduce you to Jesus, teach you right from wrong, love you beyond words, protect you and show you the power of God through my life. Instead you were the ones to teach me. You loved me beyond my faults, remained steady in the midst of life's changes, made many unspoken sacrifices, exemplify humility and forgiveness, demonstrated obedience like I've never seen, and allowed me so many do overs. You've had a front row seat to a marriage, although not perfect, managed to hold tight to Jesus and our covenant. It is my prayer that your marriage will be cemented with Jesus at the center and you will experience his grace, love, and favor like never before. May the word within these pages be a blessing to you as you navigate through the unchartered territories of marriage and make yours your own.

My husband, my love, Eliseo Sr (ECS):
    The exact words in my high school yearbook were "Hopes to run off w/ and marry ECS". My hopes and fantasy came true! I was happiest with you back then and still am.

You rescue me from life's' storms, help me in ways that are unmentionable and love me with all of you. We've grown together, gained experience from our mistakes, laughed until we cried, and learned to lean into one another in situations that would have many others running. With God's guidance you've superseded the husband of my dreams, and I'm grateful that he chose you to find me. I love you my dear heart from Westlawn to beyond!

The Ladies:

"Prince Charming" isn't only for the storybooks, he exists if you allow him to find you. Find the real you, the woman you were created to be, before the hurt and pain, without the self-esteem issues, disruptions of life, absent the selfish ambition, and pride. You are confident, fierce, and a powerhouse for God. It doesn't matter if you've never seen the perfect marriage modeled or someone to mentor you into the flawless wife. NEVER stop hoping for it. NEVER stop working at it, NEVER stop trusting God for it!

About the Book

Recipes and Direction: At the beginning of each chapter I have incorporated a fun play on words, these simple words are thought to be crucial to the existence of a marriage. The directions serve as a starting point to blend into your marriage and create success.

Ingredients: I believe these are 7 significant attributes that are an inherent part of a marriage. Tending to these ingredients or lack thereof can generally lead to success or detriment of a union.

Simmer: At the conclusion of each chapter you will find food for thought, or action steps that you can slowly take to implement positive change within your marriage.

Prayer: A powerful tool that when utilized appropriately and consistently can be the lifeline that joins a couple's hearts together and seals the desires of your heart over your marriage. Prayer changes things and it changes people, if all is well, prayer fortifies it, and if you need help in an area, prayer could be the key to changing it.

COOKBOOK

FOREWORD BY
Henry Fernandez

Denisha Sanchez just may have cooked up the perfect recipe for having a successful marriage in this delightful book she has titled, *Rice & Beans and Collard Greens.* At least it's a recipe that has worked well for her and her husband, Eliseo, now for over 30 years—most likely because they've drawn from God's recipe book, the Bible, using precise measurements of the key ingredients, including Faith, Communication, Sex, Perseverance, Godly Purpose, Fun, and Finance.

In her dedication to her husband, Denisha's words tell much of their story: "You rescue me from life's storms, help me in ways that are unmentionable and love me with all of you." These are words that mirror those of the Apostle, who wrote in 1 Peter 3:7, "Husbands, you in turn must treat your wives with tenderness, viewing them as feminine partners who deserve to be honored, for they are co-heirs with you of the '*divine* grace of life,' so that nothing will hinder your prayers" (*The Passion Translation*). And to her children, she so confidently writes: "You've had a front-row seat to a marriage, although not perfect, managed to hold tight to Jesus and our covenant."

"Almost everyone enjoys an elaborate meal at a five-star restaurant, however only a few experience the intricate details that are fused into the menu selection, meat and produce assortment, and an actual course completion," she writes, adding that in the process of preparation dishes perhaps become broken, the air conditioning system may not work adequately, food may possibly boil over, and may inevitably get stepped on. "Yet, through it all the Executive Chef never loses sight of his vision of the final presentation."

Denisha Sanchez serves up a delightful yet, rewarding meal—cooked from a God-prepared recipe that, if properly applied, can produce great results in any marriage. She is so right—our Executive Chef, our heavenly Father who, Himself, ordained the union of marriage, "whispers over the ingredients. We are His project, His pure elements, the raw components that He chose to mold into a complete meal to feed others."

I join with her in extending an invitation to come to the table, pull up a chair and enjoy this delicious meal!

APPETIZER
About Us

Looking at the big picture we had nothing in common other than the fact that we were both born in the 70's. Everything about us couldn't be more different, as different as all the unevenly match assortment of appetizers on a sampler plate in your local restaurant. After all, who puts buffalo chicken wings with an egg roll on the same plate? At least that's what I thought!

He's Puerto Rican, a "PK" (Pastor's Kid), who grew up with seven siblings in a Pentecostal household. I am African American and Cape Verdean (you may need to google it), with four sisters, growing up with a single mother and grandmother, attending the local Baptist church with neighbors. He's a risk taker, who loves movies and enjoys rice and beans with oxtails. To no surprise, I am not the risk-taker; more calculated in thought, rather read a book, big on veggies, and no beef or pork please. He said, "When I first saw her at the middle school dance, I knew she would be my wife", to the contrary I was more captivated with the music and having fun with friends. Time would pass from that initial school encounter, events would take place, people would come and go; but nothing could prevent the preparation of this fancy feast.

To sit down at the table and calculate how this peculiar couple would make it to over 3 decades together (at the time of this writing) can only be summed up in two words... God's grace! Surely, God who orchestrated this duo had a marvelous plan. He, as the Executive Chef of our life, looked over all the ingredients in his cupboard and decided to conjure up something special, but not before he washed off a few harmful pesticides from the collard greens, seasoning the rice and beans just right, and allowing all the ingredients to cook to perfection.

Almost everyone enjoys an elaborate meal at a five-star restaurant, however only a few experience the intricate details that are fused into the menu selection, meat and produce assortment, and an actual course completion. In the process of preparation dishes perhaps become broken, the air conditioning system may not work adequately, the possibility of items boiling over, and toes getting stepped on can be inevitable, yet through it all the Executive Chef never loses sight of his vision of the final presentation. "For I know the plans I have for you, declares the LORD, plans for welfare and not for evil, to give you a future and a hope" (Jeremiah 29:11 ESV), the Chef whispers over the ingredients.

We are his project, his pure elements, the raw components that he chose to mold into a complete meal to feed others. Using our story and the parts of it that we found to be significant in our marriage we openly share in expectation that everyone who pulls up to the table and picks up their fork will eat. Enjoy!

INGREDIENT 1
FAITH

Who's Doing the Shopping?

Recipe: Faith Fondue

Ingredient:

1 pound of peace

7 tablespoons of trust

2 quarts agreement

8 ounces of commitment

Directions:

Combine peace and trust. Slowly blend in agreement until bond is formed. Cover with a layer of commitment and serve immediately.

"To everything there is a season, and a time to every purpose under the heaven: A time to be born, a time to die; a time to plant, and a time to pluck up that which is planted; A time to kill, and a time to heal; a time to break down, and a time to build up; A time to weep, and a time to laugh; a time to mourn, and a time to dance; A time to cast away stones, and a time to gather stones together; a time to embrace, and a time to refrain from embracing;
A time to get, and a time to lose; a time to keep, and a time to cast away;
A time to rend, and a time to sew; a time to keep silence, and a time to speak; A time to love, and a time to hate; A time of war, and a time of peace." Eccl 3: 1-8 KJV

Just as a farmer knows the precise time of year to plant, prune and harvest his crop, a chef knows which flavors to add and which will not be necessary for a meal to taste scrumptious. The farmer recognizes in what climate to place each vegetable in order for it to grow to complete maturity similarly a chef understands the proper temperature to cook or simmer the entrée. Farmers are aware that collard greens are cool season vegetables often planted in late summer or early autumn and grow best in moist, fertile soil. They are a hearty plant that can withstand severe weather conditions and are frost tolerant. In fact, the frost actually improves the flavor of the collard green, going through a frost or cold seasons can strengthen you as a couple. Although they are a strong crop, they

 going through a frost or cold seasons can strengthen you as a couple

are still susceptible to some common pest, disease, and weeds scripture tells us, "So watch yourself! The person who thinks he can stand against sin had better watch that he does not fall into sin!" (I Cor. 10:12 NLV). Greens need plenty of space to grow before they reach their prime and are selected for harvest. You may be wondering what cultivating crops and the process of produce has to do with a book about a bi-racial couple maintaining a healthy marriage, and the ingredient FAITH. Let me explain. Each of us had to undergo our own process of growth, withstanding storms, and entering cool seasons of our life before we could be selected by the chef and prepared for the main course.

We realized that everything that we had gone through individually prepared us for the road ahead, and we were placed in the proper climate. Eliseo had to survive the divorce of his parents and watch the effects of that on his family. He had his share of unrestrained relationships and a stretch in the drug game. He was exposed to the weeds of life until he struck destiny. At the same time, I was navigating through my own garden full of rocks and unfertilized soil before I was properly fit to be picked. Certainly, growing up in a family of single unwed mothers presented a challenge to become something I had not seen.

When we met not only were cultures going to collide, but life experiences would brew up a pot of potential disaster had the chef not watched over the stove with a careful eye.

Before a meal can be stirred up, someone has to do the shopping, we decided to do it together. When we first met, Eliseo's family was in the midst of his parent's separation. He was broken and had nothing much to bring to the supermarket, let alone add any commentary for what should be on the shopping list. We were young, but knew we had to forge ahead, otherwise the cupboards would remain left bare. No one wants to encounter the crowds in the grocery store, especially when you really never wanted to be there in the first place.

Have you ever walked into the store knowing your budget was low, you're in the mood for steak or lobster and you barely have enough money for peanut butter and jelly? That was how our first few years together were. We begin dating in high school, therefore, we had to be brave enough to sustain the opinions of people that didn't think we should be dating. Moreover, we were not from the same tribe. Compile that with enduring the emotions of the high school crowd, the drama it brings and family difficulty. We were hearty plants that could withstand severe weather conditions. As difficult as some of the experiences may have seemed, they created a foundation of fertile soil. We became rooted in our relationship and stronger in our FAITH, so when the storms of life occurred and the unthinkable or unexpected happened as a couple, we could tolerate the frost.

Despite adversity, we managed to hold our heads up

high and walk into the crowded grocery store, hand in hand, with a smile on our faces, pushing the shopping cart together. As we traveled up and down each aisle looking for the deals of life, we were convinced that the chef was going to create a great masterpiece of a dish regardless of what ingredients we selected. We made the most out of what was handed to us. Carefully we looked for the bargains of life, enjoying the simple things, like walks on the beach with $1.00 ice cream cones. The value of doing the shopping together despite adversity prepared us for a life of staying in the store, remaining planted in the ground no matter how much frost we had to suffer. We recognized the game of life was better together no matter how low our budget. You must do the shopping together holding firm to your FAITH, knowing that the good Chef is actively crafting a chef-d'oeuvre for us to enjoy.

After dating for six years we finally made the big step of marriage. Initially I was frightened by the idea for many reasons, most notable the lack of support of a few family members, who believed us to be too young, or perhaps believed we should wait to find the one of same

> Big faith is always required to venture into unobserved territory.

ethnicity, despite the track record of six years of dating. The primary fear factor was that we hadn't seen very many successful healthy marriages to imitate. It's a challenge to become a successful young husband or wife when you don't have a mentor to mimic, someone to bounce things off of or anyone to instruct you in the appropriate way of being a man's greatest cheerleader or a woman's protector. Big faith is always required to venture into unobserved territory. All those concerns, coupled with that fact that our relationship had its share of ups and downs, was petrifying. God had to work on my heart, gently washing away the pesticide of doubt, and softly massaging into my mind that a marriage with Jesus in the center would blossom, be healthy and grow well. Therefore, on an extremely hot summer day in 1994, we took the first of many huge leaps of FAITH and tied the knot.

A few years after being married we made the commitment to serve the Lord wholeheartedly. The Chef's plan was beginning to take form. With nine years under our belt, we dove into ministry together becoming Sous Chefs. As Sous-Chef of the cuisine, we realized that we were second in command in the kitchen, (the person ranking next after the Executive Chef) and we began prepping for a life of availability, doing whatever our hands could do.

Things were going excellent; within a short period of time we were on a path to greatness, working in ministry and wonderful careers. Soon after we purchased our first home, we received the beautiful blessing with the birth of our son. We had been shopping together for years now and the grocery store trips seemed to be effortless. We knew the aisle, the things each other preferred and could almost quote the item prices. Trips to the store were delightful, we barely noticed the crowds or the long lines at check out. Unfortunately, as we approached aisle 11, we were taken by complete surprise, in the form of two miscarriages following the birth of our son. It would cause us to activate that FAITH ingredient like never before.

It seemed like the force of the shopping cart was hitting us right in the middle of our abdomens. After managing to recover from the initial shock of not one but two losses, our FAITH enabled us to regain our footing placing our trust in God. We prayed and waited for 8 long years. God was faithful and on one beautiful spring morning, after the frost had disappeared, our little girl named none other than **FAITH** JESSIE entered this world. Again, the Chief Chef was beginning to cook up something exclusive. Had we not continued to shop together; we may have never known what the finished product would be.

The birth of our daughter taught us that our FAITH walk together would be filled with moments of joy, peace, confusion and muddled thinking, however, with each little step forward in our journey we gained strength and assurance that we would ultimately reach our destination. We tried to enjoy the journey and not allow the mishaps to completely destroy us along the way. Doubt would arise and uncertainty set in sometimes, but God does his greatest work often in the midst of our ambiguity. One thing was for sure, our inability to make sense of things did not stop God from moving. It is similar to the farmer planting collards, by FAITH he places a few seeds in the ground. It is undefined exactly how much crop will be yielded from the seeds, but the farmer evidently continues to nurture and wait patiently, anticipating product from his field. The cultivator continues to walk by FAITH, not by sight (2 Cor. 5:7 KJV). He trusts the process as he proceeds to weed, pluck, prune steadily waiting for the manifestation. That is how we are instructed to activate our FAITH, no matter how big or small, at times you may feel confused but never doubt the hand of God. After two miscarriages we were perplexed but realized that we were never alone, likewise the disciples became boggled at times, most notably, when they couldn't cast out the demon in the boy and Jesus responded to them with a great FAITH pep talk.

[14] When they arrived at the bottom of the hill, a huge crowd was waiting for them. A man came and knelt before Jesus and said, [15] "Sir, have mercy on my son, for he is mentally deranged and in great trouble, for he often falls into the fire or into the water; [16] so I brought him to your disciples, but they couldn't cure him."

[17] Jesus replied, "Oh, you stubborn, faithless people! How long shall I bear with you? Bring him here to me." [18] Then Jesus rebuked the demon in the boy and it left him, and from that moment the boy was well.

[19] Afterwards the disciples asked Jesus privately, "Why couldn't we cast that demon out?"

[20] "Because of your little faith," Jesus told them. "For if you had faith even as small as a tiny mustard seed, you could say to this mountain, 'Move!' and it would go far away. Nothing would be impossible" (Matt 17: 14-20 TLB).

FAITH is an ingredient that a marriage cannot survive without. FAITH will move the mountains of despair, hopelessness, and dejection out of a relationship. There are many mountains that couples face today, whether it be technology interference, decline in sexual intimacy, emotional infidelity, money issues, lack of trust or selfishness. FAITH can speak to those situations. FAITH is trust in the process without the presence of evidence. It is certain even when you can't see the situation improving. FAITH believes that God is fixing it, even if it takes some time and requires a huge amount of pruning and plucking. FAITH believes that he or she will change, days will get better and together with God we will win!

"NOW Faith is the substance of things hoped for the evidence of things not seen" (Hebrews 11:1 KJV)

Simmer (FAITH is vision)

1. Do you have a vision for your marriage?

2. What steps are you taking toward achieving success in your marriage?

3. Write down three things you believe will contribute to the strengthen of faith/vision in your marriage?

Prayer

Father, we believe that you have put us together. At times we make decisions prematurely or get discouraged in the process yet at the end of the day we made a promise to our spouse; a promise that should be honored therefore when difficulties arise we lean on our faith in you to see us through. We put our trust in you to help our marriage grow fonder each day. We believe our marriage is worth fighting for and stand committed to one another. Thank you for keeping us in peace and your steady hand that rest upon our union. In Jesus name, Amen!

INGREDIENT 2
COMMUNICATION
Finding the Right Ingredient

Recipe: Communication Casserole

Ingredients:

2 gallons of listening

1 quart of understanding

1 pint of courtesy

4 cups of love

Directions:

Place courtesy in a large bowl, add listening and allow to chill for 30 minutes. Combine love and understanding. Serve warm or cooled, never hot.

"Even fools are thought wise when they keep silent; with their mouths shut, they seem intelligent"
Proverbs 17:28 (NLT)

There are several ways to communicate, verbally, non-verbally, with one's facial expressions, eye contact or lack thereof, a gesture or touch. When cooking together or as sous-chefs partnered with the Lord, it is especially important to follow the directions of communication precisely.

If a chef's recipe recommends using two cups of water and you use one cup of milk or you decide to eliminate ingredients completely, that could prove disastrous to the outcome of your dish. When my husband and I first met I really only knew how to make breakfast and lunch. The only edible dinner recipe I had up my sleeve was lasagna, nothing spectacular, it consisted of box pasta, jar sauce, ground meat and some cheese, but I won my honey over, and with a Kraft recipe, we started on a life long journey of dining together over many meals. Some were hits and many were misses along the way. Generally, he ate whatever was put in front of him, but the greatest kitchen fiasco was inevitably over my inability to make Puerto Rican style "rice and beans". Now this dish, as simple as it may sound, requires several components (even the spices and seasonings necessitate prepping), then the ingredients must be placed in the exact order, and finally, no matter how great of an effort to follow the secret formula, the rice was doomed without the proper lid to fit the perfect pot.

In spite of my Mother-in-law's patience and persistence to teach me, my efforts to master the family formula were futile. After years of several botched attempts, I eventually surrendered and purchased a rice cooker. Our future "rice and beans" dishes would consist of white rice and red beans on the side, or "fine-tuned" yellow rice with vegetables done my way. Did my inability to make the perfect side dish to his meat make me a failure as a wife? Of course not, but the kitchen was certainly the battlefield for both of us to be left as casualties of "word" wars several times. It would take some time before we put into practice "A gentle answer turns away wrath, but hard words stir up anger." (Proverbs 15:1 NIV)

During the early years of our marriage and beyond, I had to learn how to clearly speak with my husband about my desire to please and feed him. I genuinely wanted to serve him "Rice and Beans" that reminded him of his Momma's cooking but the frustration that would arise within me each time he requested it was a pure segue for a communication melt-down. How could this happen? I just have to cook, and he just has to eat, therefore let me elaborate on exactly how the conversation would ensue.

(her) Babe ... what do you want to eat?

(him) I'm really in the mood for some steak with "rice and beans".

(her) Ughhh... you know I really don't feel like making that, it never comes out right. The rice is always seasoned great and mushy, or not seasoned correctly and too hard.

(him) That's not true babe, it comes out alright.

(her) See you said "alright". I know that's not what you really wanted to say... It doesn't taste quite like your Mom's so it's alright.

(him) Fine babe, don't make the rice and beans.

(her) You don't even appreciate my efforts.

(him) I'm just saying, its fine! Whatever babe, I'll eat cereal.

(her) What did you say?

(him) Nothing, babe nothing (followed by silence and loud sighs).

I did mention this was in the early years, right? Pre- rice cooker? When you are in your early 20's and newly married, mole hills quickly become mountains. Nevertheless, the communication on both our parts needed some real work. There were plenty of unmet expectations. We each had to learn the way the other responded best to our feedback or requests and certainly over the years we had to become more skilled at listening to understand opposed to listening to respond. Frequently, the mouth does not always say the right thing at the right time.

Knowing each other's heart is an important aspect of communication because the brain doesn't always accurately articulate the very thing the heart is trying to convey. A beautiful biblical example of a couple that displays the measure of the heart and not the head is Elkanah and Hannah. Elkanah loved Hannah dearly, and although his words seemed to articulate that love in an unorthodox way, she did not allow that to deter her from feeling his true sense of compassion.

Now Elkanah had two wives Peninnah and Hannah, which was typical in those days. Peninnah bore his children and Hannah had not. Peninnah was antagonistic toward Hannah which made Hannah incredibly sad. Elkanah, being a caring covering of his wife was not put out by her pain or sadness but rather tried to comfort her in word and deed. He would give double portion to display his love, and in essence, speaking to her destiny that your future will one day include more than just you; you will have children that will partake in this portion. He followed up his giving with his "words of comfort" "Why are you crying, Hannah?" Elkanah would ask. "Why aren't you eating? Why be downhearted just because you have no children? You have me—isn't that better than having ten sons?" (1 Samuel 1:8 NLT). To some reading his statement, the words may appear to be full of reckless rhetoric or an irresponsible way to respond to a sorrowful and dejected wife, but for Hannah she knew the sincerity of his heart. In spite of how the brain transposed the words she used those words as motivation to rise up, eat, drink, and get in motion to see the priest for her next move.

Now, I'm not insinuating that one shouldn't give great thought and consideration to the way they speak to the other, "Good people think before they answer, but the wicked speak evil without ever thinking" (Proverbs 15:28 CEV). I am simply suggesting that communication is more than the way in which words are spoken. Communication is a matter of the heart and involves maturity as well.

Communication is more than simple conversation it requires comprehension and listening with your whole heart in every aspect and striving to understand more than being understood. It takes two to tango, therefore never hit the other the way you've been hit. It is still noble to retreat and beneficial to remain in a sweet quiet place. I am definitely not implying the angry silent treatment, and mature people know and value the difference. "Be ye angry, and sin not: let not the sun go down upon your wrath" (Ephesians 4:26 KJV). The scripture also, declares that "Every wise woman buildeth her house; But the foolish plucketh it down with her own hands" (Proverbs 14:1 ASV), the battle will continue as long as bullets are traded. When it is noted that a fierce exchange is about to ensue, I'd like to invoke the "shut it down" rule. For example, when your husband is in a "foul mood" or you're "caught up in your feelings", a wise point of view is to "shut it down". In other words, don't keep adding fuel to the fire. Press the "Mute" button on your lips and hold your peace.

Our conversations, regardless of the issue, must be integrated with basic principles of compassion, love, discernment, and timing. Unedifying conversations or "heated fellowship" in the kitchen during meal preparation time was a frequent occurrence. Our "rice and beans" sagas pale in comparison to those more crucial topics, such as child rearing and finances. Despite the intensity of the subject matter, the same basic values of communication must apply.

When communicating as a couple, we need to remember that words have power and can hurt, once they are spoken, they cannot be retrieved no matter how hard you try.

16

Over the years, I messed up several pots of rice and beans. My husband could already notice that I was defeated. He could have added

 remember that words have power and can hurt, once they are spoken, they cannot be retrieved no matter how hard you try

salt to my wounded spirit and demolished all my efforts with mean and hateful words, but he chose to build me up with encouragement and words that would increase my belief in myself to try again.

As the opportunity arises to either "heal" or engage in "heated fellowship" the best remedy is operating from a place of love and or remain in silence. Why would you spend so many years of life building a house, then only to burn it down? That is what unsympathetic, careless, inconsiderate words do to a marriage. The result is catastrophic. We had to learn, and are still learning, how to combat the negligent side of communication; we frequently remind ourselves that the way we speak to each other is a direct reflection of how we want God to view our love toward him. "Let the words of my mouth and the meditation of my heart be acceptable in your sight, O LORD, my rock and my redeemer" (Psalms 19:14 ESV).

"Do not use harmful words, but only helpful words, the kind that build up and provide what is needed, so that what you say will do good to those who hear you"
(Ephesians 4:29 GNT)

Simmer (Communication)

1. Do you THINK (is it True, Helpful, Inspiring, Necessary and Kind) before you speak?

2. Have you examined your body language as part of your communication (what are the unspoken words you speak)?

3. Do you listen to understand or respond?

Prayer

Loving Lord, I thank you for allowing me the privilege to speak life and communicate with love to my spouse. Equip us with words that build up, encourage, and bring comfort. May my words speak hope, to all those that hear them, especially my husband/wife. Father, I understand that the way I communicate with my spouse is a direct reflection of how I see you and perceive you at work in their life. With patience train me to choose my words carefully and articulate them effectively that they produce growth. Thank you, Lord, for helping us to be keepers of your word in speech and deed. In Jesus name, Amen!

INGREDIENT 3
SEX

Let's Start Cooking

Recipe: Sex Souffle

Ingredients:

1 teaspoon hot sauce (optional)

¼ cup of oil

1 quart of strawberries

2 cups melted chocolate

½ gallon of emotional awareness

Directions:

Preheat the oven to 500 (most oven's maximum point), allow oil to heat, and slowly sift in emotional awareness. Hot sauce may be added to taste. In a microwavable bowl melt chocolate and dip strawberries until covered.

"Let him kiss me with the kisses of his mouth! For your love is better than wine. Draw me after you; let us run. The king has brought me into his chambers."
Song of Solomon 1:2,4 ESV

Let's be honest. Sex is incredibly fun in the bonds of marriage. God created it for marriage and the pleasures from it are phenomenal! To say that sexual intimacy with your spouse is not entertaining or fun would be a lie.

However, being created as sensual beings comes with a price. In a world that is constantly evolving and advancing at the speed of light, with sexuality at the front of almost every industry and most aspects of things, it's virtually effortless to detach from your compass of life.

The reality is that with every sexually driven commercial, pornography at the touch of a button and body enhancement readily available, it is extremely easy to lose touch with realism and forget the genuine confines of what sex between a husband and wife should be like.

From the beginning of time man struggled with being alone and trying to find the perfect life partner. Throughout the bible it is noticed that a man's great down fall was attributed to his inability to control his innate passion to be fulfilled sexually. "Late one afternoon about dusk, David got up from his couch and was walking around on the roof of the royal palace. From there he watched a woman taking a bath, and she was very beautiful to look at. David sent word to inquire about her, and someone told him, "This is Eliam's daughter Bathsheba, the wife of Uriah the Hittite, isn't it?" So David sent some messengers, took her from her home, and she went to him, and he had sex with her. (She had been consecrating herself following her menstrual separation) Then she returned to her home" (2 Samuel 11: 2-4 ISV).

Clearly this was not God's intent when he designed marriages. God's strategy was that the two should not only survive but thrive, and he laid out the perfect plan.

Man shouldn't be alone I will make a helpmate, And the Lord God said, "It isn't good for man to be alone; I will make a companion for him, a helper suited to his needs" (Genesis 2:18 TLB) what I put together let no one come between, "Therefore what God has joined together, man must not separate" (Mark 10:9 HCS) the two will become one, "That is why a man leaves his father and mother and is united with his wife, and they become one" (Genesis 2:24 GNT), finally sex is good and should remain solely between the two.

With those boundaries in motion, let the exquisite days and nights commence. Hold up! Only one additional caveat, they shall remain one flesh "to death do they part". This is a big order. How can we make the most of our erotic time together and genuinely keep that passion going just between the two of us for our entire life? Although it may sound extreme, it undoubtedly is possible. Just play by a few simple rules; number one keep it honest, and trustworthy with God's word at the center and the primary focus of intimacy.

Thankfully, when God specially designed me and my husband for each other he specifically took note of our sex appeal for one another. God fashioned us extremely compatible, we more than enjoy our intimate time together. The key word being "intimate" because sex in a marriage can be more than just physical.

Throughout our marriage it hasn't always been fierce fire and ecstasy. Although the stove is always present in the kitchen it is not always lit. It can be problematic to begin cooking when the space is cluttered, or dirty dishes are in the sink. Inevitably you will need a pot or spoon, and if they are unclean it only slows up the process. Certainly, over the years as the pressures of life mount, demanding schedules, perhaps health issues, add in the birth of children and body changes, feeling sexy at times is not always top priority.

As a woman, you can show me you love me better than you can tell me. What you deposit during the day will determine your withdrawal at night. For the man, anytime, any day, anywhere, any way is perfect!

A lesson we learned early in our marriage was you must not let the fire go out. If that happens, it is often difficult if not near impossible, to rekindle. I recall as newlyweds our first apartment had a "gas" stove. For those that are unfamiliar with this antique appliance, here's a quick tutorial. On the stove top are four burners, each one possesses their own "pilot" and the pilot is what feeds the gas to the "ignition" and ultimately produces the fire. If the pilot goes out, then you must manually light it with a match.

The biggest challenge in cooking with gas is figuring out how to appropriately adjust the flame. It takes precision, a steady hand and patience at first, if the flame is too high you are sure to scorch your meal instantly and on the other hand, if it is too low, it's comparable to watching

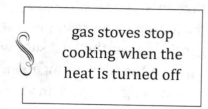

gas stoves stop cooking when the heat is turned off

paint dry, long and boring. You must find the right heat! The main thing to remember is gas stoves stop cooking when the heat is turned off.

Patience and a steady hand are essential before you can actually start cooking. My husband and I were fortunate to have been blessed with 10 years together as a couple prior to our son entering our world, therefore, unconstrained, and ferocious was not tricky at all. The time when it was just the two of us produced the much-needed patience and steadiness that would be necessary to prep us for what would happen the year of his birth. The same year Eliseo Jr. was born, we purchased our first home and my husband started a new job.

As more responsibility began to be added, our daily life appeared to become more intense and the spontaneity and freshness of our relationship seemed to be dim. It was as if a "pilot" or two had gone out. We realized that as a couple we were fading into the mundane, so we pulled out the matches, sparked a fire and initiated what we call "keeping it hot". Now "keeping it hot" is not "date night" in fact it's not a date at all. It has nothing to do with a night of the week and actually doesn't require going out but what it does demand is being physically and emotionally present.

"Keeping it hot" is what keeps the cooking process from slipping into an unexciting everyday routine. It reminds us that once you start cooking, you must remain mindful that the journey is more important than the destination. It's the gentle pat on the backside while maneuvering your way through the kitchen together. It's being intentional about maintaining the spark in your eye when you see each other, or the sweet kiss that Solomon was referring to when you arrive home or meet up in the street *"Let him kiss me with the kisses of his mouth! For your love is better than wine. Draw me after you; let us run. The king has brought me into his chambers"* (Song of Solomon 1:2,4 ESV).

I've heard it said, "what you won't do, someone else will do freely". With those words in the back of my mind, playing it safe in our marriage was not an option. By playing it safe, you become complacent and begin to overlook each other's desires and take one another for granted. Your marriage gives way to unexceptional, stale and commonplace. The stove grows cold and conventional. Anything left unattended will eventually gravitate to chaos. When you pay no attention to the things on the stove, they will quickly begin to bubble over or burn.

If your kitchen is cluttered and those dirty dishes are piling up in the form of a nagging spouse, financial snags, or perhaps health struggles, don't let that be the breeding ground for the "new normal". Use your skills and will power to set those burners ablaze again. It will take fortitude and tolerance at times, but don't allow someone else to slip in and do what you are not willing to work for.

Despite having a newborn and a demanding work

schedule, we had to recognize that the initial lust we had for each other must be converted into love and staying power. Note that staying power will mandate stamina and creativity. Life is full of swift transitions and can get busy quickly, therefore be ready to openly talk about what each of you desires physically and find a common ground. Do not allow days or weeks to sneak by without acknowledging each other's presence and needs. Early on in your marriage use those days to discover your wants and pleasures. If you have been married for some time, evolve and experiment mentally and physically.

God desires that we have an amusing and enjoyable life; intimacy with your spouse is a portion of that abundance. The intimacy for one may involve flirting with the other, sending a love note or drawing a warm bath. The closeness may be shared over a dinner, walking hand in hand or slow dancing in the kitchen while you make French toast. The important thing is not to allow the affection that you once shared as a couple become a thing of the past. Don't permit physical or emotional distance to overtake your desire to be with each other. Familiar and comfortable will seep into your relationship in the same way as being unaware that the pilot to the gas stove it out; it's lethal. Extinguished pilot lights can release carbon monoxide (CO). The dangerous fumes will fill the air of your home without your knowledge and suffocate the life out of each of you. Be vigilant of these vapors and keep the kitchen clutter free; agree that tenderness, caring and remaining attentive will dominate your intimacy.

Protect yourself from intimacy killers. Do you want to have a marriage where your spouse comes home, kisses you on the cheek, searches the pots for what is for dinner, then proceeds to interact the remainder of the evening with the intimacy killers? Most notable killers are the internet, TV, or phone. Beware of those tendencies which can potentially hurt couples. This type of behavior is a real trap of the enemy. If you can stay ahead of him your chances of survival are great. The bible declares there is nothing new under the sun, therefore his tricks and traps have remained the same for centuries.

Amazingly enough before marriage Satan tempted couples towards premarital sex, but in marriage, his energy focuses on tempting them to not have sex. Satan wants to hinder a married couple's intimacy through lack of sex. It is so easy to say, remain committed to God and each other, ignore the adversary's ploy and he will leave "Submit yourselves, then, to God. Resist the devil, and he will flee from you" (James 4:7 NIV), however it takes more than simply overlooking such tactics. Whatever you give your attention to, it will give you direction. Therefore, a couple must remain diligent in focusing on each other, often times placing the interest and needs of the other person before you own.

> Whatever you give your attention to, it will give you direction.

Sex in a marriage requires deep connection even when you don't desire to connect. To turn your back on your spouse physically, mentally, and emotionally is an invitation for disaster. I do realize that certain situations have made it difficult to step into the realm of romance. If emotionally a spouse has been harmed or betrayed, turning up the love odometer may take a lot of prayer, conversation, and perhaps even counseling for healing. But I can assure you, that your marriage is worth fighting for. If busyness and loss of priority has caused confusion in the bedroom and the sex life is fizzling, recommit to "keeping it hot". Take baby steps toward turning up the love dial and start cooking again.

"Love is not measured by how many times you touch each other, but by how many times you reach each other."
— Unknown

Simmer (Sex)

1. Can you identify what peaks your spouse sexual interest?

2. How will you continue to "keep it hot"?

3. What steps are you taking to protect your marriage from intimacy killers?

Prayer

Dear Father, we recognize that it is you that has put us together and we desire to please you even in the most intimate times that we share together. Prepare us for the journey of monogamy. Show us how to remain committed, connected and engaged with our spouse. Allow us to keep romance and spontaneity alive in our relationship. We thank you for keeping our eyes on alert for distraction and we are discerning of each other's needs. We come up against intimacy killers and proclaim a thriving and sexually healthy marriage in the mighty name of Jesus. Amen!

INGREDIENT 4
PERSERVERANCE

Honey, I Burnt the Meal

Recipe: Perseverance Parfait

Ingredients:

1 pound of focus

2 pints of passion

1 tablespoon of steadfastness

4 ounces of patience

Directions:

Mix together all ingredients except passion. Spoon into cups and chill overnight. Once completely cooled top with passion.

"Brothers and sisters, I do not consider myself yet to have taken hold of it. But one thing I do: Forgetting what is behind and straining toward what is ahead, [14]I press on toward the goal to win the prize for which God has called me heavenward in Christ Jesus" Philippians 3:13-14 NIV.

Have you ever heard the old adage "when it rains it pours"? Similar is the phrase "the harder you try the harder it gets". Life can be unfair and with filled with many sharp turns, and as a result of its swiftness you may experience a wide array of emotions. There may be times of joy, peace, contentment, or anger, hurt, disappointment and frustration. Often times the moments of greatest discomfort bring about the greatest change. I can't promise you many things, but this one thing is sure, the only certain thing in life is change. If you are married long enough, you may have to endure a generous amount of change and challenges and then be forced to become acquainted with the gamut of feelings that accompany those transitions. Change can give birth to perseverance or indolence.

When we look at the life of Job (Job 1:13-22 – CEV) we observe a great biblical account that illustrates an image of pronounced perseverance, through it all he continued to praise God.

¹³ "Job's sons and daughters were having a feast in the home of his oldest son, ¹⁴ when someone rushed up to Job and said, "While your servants were plowing with your oxen, and your donkeys were nearby eating grass, ¹⁵ a gang of Sabeans[a] attacked and stole the oxen and donkeys! Your other servants were killed, and I was the only one who escaped to tell you."

¹⁶ That servant was still speaking, when a second one came running up and saying, "God sent down a fire that killed your sheep and your servants. I am the only one who escaped to tell you."

¹⁷ Before that servant finished speaking, a third one raced up and said, "Three gangs of Chaldeans[b] attacked and stole your camels! All of your other servants were killed, and I am the only one who escaped to tell you."

¹⁸ That servant was still speaking, when a fourth one dashed up and said, "Your children were having a feast and drinking wine at the home of your oldest son, ¹⁹ when suddenly a windstorm from the desert blew the house down, crushing all of your children. I am the only one who escaped to tell you."

²⁰ When Job heard this, he tore his clothes and shaved his head because of his great sorrow. He knelt on the ground, then worshiped God ²¹ and said:

"We bring nothing at birth;
we take nothing
    with us at death.

The LORD alone gives and takes.
Praise the name of the LORD!"

²² In spite of everything, Job did not sin or accuse God of doing wrong."

No one in their right mind could fathom the anguish that had entered Job's life in an instant. How could he experience such suffering and yet remain what appeared to be unscathed? After all, Job immediately had to face a "new normal". This is precisely how you may be feeling as you read this book; that life has been cruel and hit you with one devastating blow after the next. The loaded question is, will you fold to failure or rise triumphantly as fearless?

Life is no longer a balancing act and the bestselling self-help book may be of no assistance in trying to put all of the pieces back together again. In fact, humpty dumpty has fallen off the wall for the final time. You may have been saying to yourself, "I'm done and done for real", "marriage counseling isn't going to help", "she or he is never going to change", or "this is the last time he or she hurts me this way". Well, I'd like to offer a word of encouragement, if perhaps Job's life was not enough.

There comes a time in every marriage, when one or both of the individuals feel themselves outgrowing certain things (it may be friends, a career, your home) and change is necessary. We felt that way after spending nearly a decade at the same church and almost 2 decades in the same city. We came to a fork in the road and were presented with an opportunity to relocate our family from our hometown to an entirely different region of the country. It appeared to be the answer to our prayers. It was a decision that required a vast amount of prayer and conversation. After all, we had bought our first home there, had family ties and wonderful careers. However, with each day that passed, it become clear that it was time to move. Therefore, with the house up for sale, cars packed and 2 children in tow, we were off to what we believed to be brighter days and greener pastures.

Unfortunately, the sun eventually went into hiding, blue skies became gray and the thunderstorm of life had settled upon us in our new location. Soon we found ourselves facing another daunting decision, do we stay or go? This next phase in our life was crucial, carrying with it reprieve or heavy consequences. Sadly, the outcome would lead us to the desert of life. With the hot desert sun beating down on us emotionally, physically, and financially, we watched as things shriveled away. For the first time in our marriage, my husband was unemployed, and not for a week or two, but 16 weeks total. To top it off, he couldn't collect unemployment in this new state, and I was only working a part-time job. With money running low, bills always due, and two children to feed, things were looking bleak. We were forced to seek public assistance from food pantries and Medicare for medical needs. We had to now become accustomed to a "new normal". We never felt it would be permanent, but it was necessary, scary, and overwhelming all at the same time. To think, we sold our home, left our family, gave up our jobs to now find ourselves having to eat at "Taco Tuesday" with .39 cent tacos and one large lemonade "watered down", to split between the four of us was humbling. Lack of money never really seemed to get the best of us, but this ordeal was definitely pulling at every string of our marriage. The children were young and unaware of the discomfort that their parents were facing, but the effects of our decisions were taking a toll on us personally.

Eliseo had loss approximately 25lbs and I was at an all-time low in weight and physical health. Some way, somehow, God pulled us up out of that low place, with the support from a few lifelong friends who believed in us, a couple of family members, and 2 small ministries whose Pastors showed themselves friendly. Most from the outside looking in were unaware or unbothered by our disturbance.

The real true test of your perseverance is when you realize that although money may run low, you're in between employment, family or friends may leave your side and sickness might arrive, at the end of the day all you really have is whatever relationship you have built with God and each other. We knew in our hearts regardless of what it looked like we would not quit. We were built for this and to preserve was not optional it was mandatory. In the face of adversity, we held on to this scripture "And we know that God works all things together for the good of those who love Him, who are called according to His purpose" (Roman 8:28 BSB).

> remembering in the dark what God told me in the light

This season demonstrated quite clearly that tough times will come. The ironic thing is tough times don't last; tough people do. We kept our eyes on God, never stopped praising him or thanking him even when at times we really did not feel like it. A key for me was remembering in the dark what God told me in the light.

Over the years, as my lifestyle changed, I became aware of the importance of altering behavior or modifying things to best suit the change. Sometime after being married, I chose to no longer eat beef or pork. It was a gradual change for me; no religious reason, I simply believe this to be healthier eating practice. My husband detested the idea and insisted as long as it didn't affect his meals it was a go. Little by little as I prepared our food, I would slowly eliminate certain ingredients in hopes that he wouldn't notice. Most dishes went off without a hitch, however it was the old tasty southern style collard greens that caused him to go on high alert for all future dishes. Sometimes it's just one thing that changes the way you see the future.

One day, I thought it would be a fabulous idea to alter my grandmother's collard green recipe and replace the main stable of ham hock with spices. Surely it would need a lot of doctoring up. In an effort to really let the seasonings saturate the greens, I lowered the heat and left them to simmer for far too long. I burnt the greens! With this catastrophe, and all my hard work of cutting and cleaning the produce down the drain, I now had to decide, whether to retry with smoke turkey legs, perhaps turkey bacon or eliminate this essential green from our life all together. Would I give up on cooking this dish completely? Would we starve or try again? I was committed to working hard to perk up this side dish and I worked unto I got it right! Eventually, I perfected a newly found recipe. It was a do-over of sorts, the new and improved version. Had I not been persistent and persevered this vegetable would have been eliminated completely. This certainly was a light affliction in comparison to major decisions and obstacles we had to face, and we've burned a lot of meals together over the years in the form of missed moments and dreams unfulfilled, but the key is not allowing these overlooked opportunities, to cause you to miss out on what the rest of life could offer.

God uses time and pressure to change things. When growing collards, it goes through a process of facing brutal weather conditions before it matures into a healthy stock of greens ready to be shipped off as good produce for the store. The process before we purchase these items in itself is so tumultuous that only the strong survive. Such is the same for a healthy marriage to survive the storms of life in order for a productive life of two people becoming one. Time and pressure must exist before change can take place.

> God uses time and pressure to change things.

Perseverance means even when your burnt in life like that pot of collard greens or scorched from the desert sun you still continue on. You still must make up your mind that you will walk this journey of life together no matter how messy the kitchen gets, no matter how bad the aroma or how much smoke fills the air. We were determined that no matter how sticky the pot gets, or sand kicked in our face from the fierce desert wind, we would be unmoved from our covenant with each other.

Similar to Job, we had to learn as a couple, we must persevere in the faith regardless of life's circumstance. As a couple I don't know what you will face but I am certain that this world is plagued with divorce, infidelity, conflict, substance abuse, lack of commitment and violence. Perseverance is the main ingredient that aids in the time and pressure process. It's the tireless grit that enables you to weather each storm, merged with unwavering love. It's the salve that covers ever burn or wound you may encounter along the way.

We just about lost everything in our desert season but like Job we persevered. Walking through that dry period I had to encourage myself with these words "If I lose all my money and possessions, I have lost nothing. If I lose my health, I've lost something, but if I lose my character and love toward my husband, I will have lost everything".

As with a pot of burnt greens, you start over or similarly to all the botched attempts to make rice and beans, I had to tweak the recipe and try again. Perseverance is tenacity, courage, and strength in your relationship. There may be times when you lose everything or feel like you are losing each other but you must remind yourselves that the latter will be greater, there is no quitting in you. Maya Angelou once said, "We may encounter

> You may have to change your position on some things or your locations, but you never change your mind about one another.

many defeats, but we must not be defeated". You may have to change your position on some things or your locations, but you never change your mind about one another.

We learned with every step of our marriage that the road would not always be easy and that we would cry sometime; but as sure as the sun rises in the east, brighter days would come as long as we hung in there with each other. "...Weeping may endure for a night, but joy cometh in the morning" (Psalms 30:5 KJV). No matter what comes your way hang in there together, you have what it takes to make it!

"Patience and perseverance have a magical effect before which difficulties disappear and obstacles vanish"
John Quincy Adams

Simmer (Perseverance)

1. Do you have a plan to keep going when times get rough, if so, please list your steps?

2. List key reasons why, you shouldn't give up on your marriage?

3. Thankfulness sustains us in caring for our spouse, name a few things your spouse does that you are thankful for?

Prayer

Great God show us the path that always leads to you, teach us how to trust even in difficult times. Lord, we lean not on our own understanding but continue to keep our eyes fixed on you. Thank you for never leaving us and giving us strategies to persevere and hope to hold on to. Safeguard our hearts from the desire to quit or self-sabotage. In the matchless name of Jesus, Amen.

INGREDIENT 5
GODLY PURPOSE
A Good Cook Cleans Up the Mess

Recipe: Classic Godly Goulash

Ingredients:

1-liter thankfulness

2 pints humility

4 cups knowledge

Sprinkle with the holy spirit

Directions:

Rinse and drain knowledge. Combine thankfulness and crushed humility in a jar and shake. Pour over knowledge. Sprinkle with an abundance of the holy spirit. Serve immediately.

"It is the same with my word. I send it out, and it always produces fruit.
It will accomplish all I want it to, and it will prosper everywhere I send it" Isaiah 55:11NLT

In marriage you are either growing together or apart. Growing together means each person is nurturing, cultivating, and discovering their life's purpose and how that ties into their purpose as a married couple. Often times marriages fail because couples grow apart. Growing as an individual while trying to grow as a couple is a challenge since we grow differently, and our world seems to highlight independence, self-promotion and self-importance oppose to reliance upon each other. Nevertheless, growing through things alone doesn't make you independent of the other "and the two will become one. So, they are no longer two, but one" (Mark 10:8 GNT). It allows you to mature in the marriage. Unwillingness to come together or be mature enough to disagree without losing the love is an adversary to a successful, happy, and healthy relationship. Marriage comes with compromise even during the growing.

A secret phrase that needs to be adopted by every person that enters into a marriage is "NO DIVORCE" regardless of how long it takes, or the space needed for the other to grow. Both must admit and commit to allowing these words to permanently reside in your hearts; that divorce is not an option.

Growing is not always easy because things begin to stretch and pull often times beyond your comfort zone. A great deal of work, time, attention, and environment cultivation go into the process. It is similar to planting the collard greens, the area chosen for planting should be in full sun. Seeds are planted in rows at least 3 feet apart, as the growing collards get large and need room to grow. While 60 to 75 days is an average harvest time for growing collard greens to reach maturity, the leaves can be picked at any time they are of edible size from the bottom of the large, inedible stalks. Just as each plant size, shape and cultivation period varies, so too do individuals within a marriage.

As a married couple, there are somethings in life you have to develop, study, and grow through alone. Although you are planted in the same field, permitted space to grow enhances the size of the plant.

I had to learn this the hard way. It is extremely challenging to understand how to develop as an independent thinker when you have been with the same person for more than half your life. I initially met my husband in middle school, and I feel tremendously blessed to have married my high school sweetheart. We've been privileged to go through life together for over three decades. Over those years we have undergone many of life's ups and downs, wins and losses, births, and deaths. Our lives have melted together in almost every aspect of our beings, we can finish each other's sentences, I can order for him at the restaurant, know his favorite sports teams, can prepare his preferred meals, and I especially know what turns him on and off.

We are each other's support always. We know the other's strengths and weakness, and generally agree on most things, however even at the time of writing this book, I couldn't convince him enough to write it in its entirety with me. The most amazing thing is that I became aware that God has a plan for us together and a plan for us as individuals that are joined together with him.

My husband and I came to a few crossroads as a couple and were uncertain if our marriage would be able to withstand the test of time. After dating for two years, I graduated high school and was headed off to college and he would not be relocating with me. At that time, we were unsure if we could maintain our relationship given the distance, time, space, new place, and people. As I approached my departure, of course we believed we were both totally committed, although only time and God would tell. With our best feet forward, I set forth to the dorms almost 100 miles away. The distance between us made it impossible to see each other during the week (this was before facetime, skype and other social media platforms). We did our best to make time on weekends, however, as the semesters continued and final exams approached with coarse work becoming more demanding every weekend soon became a test of our wills to hang in there with each other or fall victims to what life had to offer.

It would have been easy to let the chips fall where they may; After all, we were young and dedicated but not married.

With a taxing study schedule and no free time on my end, and the wrong people in his ear and plenty of time on his hand, would our devotion for one another withstand all odds? As only God would have it, we defied the odds, and remained loyal and committed. It was all part of God's purpose.

After one year in the dorm and being separated by distance, he decided to leave his family and friends to join me. This short one-year period set a foundation for our relationship of independence, faithfulness to each other, and a trust in God to see him work all things together for our good.

It was the start of sophomore year in college and now we were close again. Surely life was good, but a new place and new people proved to be an unhealthy concoction for my husband. Life was full of distraction for him as I tried my best to maintain focus and keep my Dean's list status while working several jobs. His only ambition was his newly found bad company. Our kitchen was getting messy and we both were not walking in the same direction, but God had a way of cleaning up the mess and helping us climb the mountain together. It was Muhammad Ali that said, "It isn't the mountains ahead to climb that wear you out; it's the pebble in your shoes". At many points each of us was worn out. During those college years, I must say I was worn out more than him. Things got tough but God's will is tougher, even when we couldn't see it or felt like giving it our all, God's plan was greater for us and our future together would be bright. I encourage you to always remember his plan is greater!

We both were learning how to walk our path separately trying to achieve our own goals but constantly allowing God to order our steps toward each other without even knowing it. We were not serving the Lord, but he was continually in our affairs. At times we felt his intervention and other days he didn't seem near or at least we were unaware, but God kept us. God's plan and purpose took us in different directions although we never separated. There were times as a couple, I still felt alone. Truly it was only the ear of God that heard many of my mid-night hour prayers. "Though my loud groaning, my flesh clings to my bones. I am like a desert owl, like an owl among the ruins. I lie awake; I am like a lone bird on a housetop" (Psalms 102: 5-7 BSB). I love this passage of scripture because I was alone crying out to God feeling like that desert owl. Many owls live alone most of the year. This living alone is called 'solitary' life. Occasionally, especially in the winter, small species of owl roost together in one area. The Owls generally have a hunting territory away from their daytime roost. All Owls are equipped with special adaptations that make them efficient predators, because their feathers hardly make any noise when they fly, and their keen eyesight allows them locate prey even on dim nights.

I was determined not to die empty or remain lonely in this relationship. I was not going to coexist in solitary confinement. I was going to use my special adaptation to efficiently defeat the enemies of our relationship. I never gave up on my man; with keen eyesight I focused in and with God as my guide and feathers hardly making a sound, we contested those negative people out of our life one by one. I gently reminded my future husband of God's purpose for his life, all the while pushing forward toward mine. This push was only because of God's presence.

I candidly recount those days as an encouragement to remind you that you might be in the midst of a dirty kitchen, with a countertop full of crumbs, sticky oil on the stove, and a sink full of dishes. Perhaps your cupboards are bare, and your kitchen seems useless without any food to prepare. That is precisely how I felt during many of my college days, that our relationship was unusable and not producing much. I had a significant other but felt very alone.

We had to invite God in to clean up the mess, he is not only the executive Chef that cleans as he goes, but he became the policy maker, managerial supervisor, and chief builder in our life. God is in the restoring business, he can repair, replace, rejuvenate, renovate, replenish, renew, and intervene right in the knick of time, if you continue to seek him through it all. You must pray and cry out to him continually despite the circumstance or events that are currently taking place. You may have to push (P.U.S.H. pray until something happens) and take flight like the owl alone in the cool dark air, but know you are equipped to defeat those predators of addiction, infidelity, lack, unruly or disobedient children, aging parents, ups and downs of life, that attempt to wear you out.

> We had to invite God in to clean up the mess

The journey may seem tireless, even larger than life sometimes, with distractions and derailments seemingly at every corner. How do you keep those tiny little pebbles from discouraging you? Be wise and keep a close eye on small things that can add up, irritate you and then ultimately attempt to destroy your journey together.

Certainly, like the owl, God had created all species unique and for their own design and his purpose, but the other extraordinary part of this story is that as a couple we were destined to be each other's help in fulfilling our Godly purpose. During those college days of struggle there were times my future husband's behavior was a bulky obstacle, but he was also my greatest support and fan. The support he offered, mentally, physically, and spiritually was immeasurable. During those periods of tremendous stress from the assignments and workload, he proved to be my biggest advocate, a shoulder to cry on, a hand to hold, the pat on the back, my courier, financier, lunch maker, and friend through it all. Unquestionable many did not believe our relationship would sustain the 100 mile distance between us, nor weather the storms of the college years and all the tension it would bring (we were a young couple, living away from the familiar with financial burdens totally dependent upon each other) however, God's plan would prevail. We continued to believe in each other and ourselves as a couple, even when no one else did. During the most difficult of times, God was yet again conditioning us for the road ahead, the road that would ultimately lead to his purpose.

God has a purpose and plan for everything under the heaven. Even if life may get messy along the way, God is not changing his mind about you and in the end you will win.

"Efforts and courage are not enough without purpose and direction" *John F. Kennedy*

Simmer (Godly Purpose)

1. Are you aware of your individual purpose?

2. As a couple, can you identify how your individual purpose works together in your marriage?

Prayer

Father, your mighty hand created me for your purpose and pleasure. The ideas you have for us are so much greater than we could imagine as a couple. Make certain your desire is in our hearts that we do not veer off the plan you have for us. Give us the discipline and strategies to stay true to our Godly purpose and we will forever live up to our full potential in you. Amen.

INGREDIENT 6
FUN

It's Dinner Time!

Recipe: Feather Light Fun Rolls

Ingredients:

pinch of laughter

1lb of love

1oz of affection

2 cups fun

Directions:

Mix ½ lb. of love, affection in with fun, then deep fry in a pinch of laughter. When cool, add remaining ½ lb. of love, roll up like a jelly roll and cut as large of slice to enjoy.

49

"A joyful heart is good medicine, but a broken spirit dries up the bones" *Proverbs 17:22 (NASB).*

A good authentic serving of rice and beans is irresistible. When all those savory ingredients are combined in one pot, it sure to taste delightful. A classic Puerto Rican rice and bean recipe calls for a secret component named "sofrito". Sofrito is a seasoning that "jazzes up" the recipe. It consists of several items and necessitates much work. A typical sofrito is made up of very finely chopped green, red, and yellow bell peppers, red onions, garlic, ground oregano, apple cider vinegar, tomato paste, water, and cilantro. Sofrito can be store bought, however when made from scratch there is no mistaking the scrumptious taste. Sofrito encompasses great effort to prepare, but necessary if you desire the little extra pop in your rice. The variety of ingredients is the perfect blend to a happy palette. Fun and laughter are the sofrito in a marriage, it gives your relationship the extra pop. Although it may require extra effort and a variety of activities nevertheless it makes for an irresistible marriage. Rice may be edible with the generic store-bought brands of sofrito, on the other hand the rice, with the bona fide homemade sofrito, is simply enchanting.

Marriage is meant to be pleasurable and exciting and

though every day won't be joy filled, a couple certainly can work at keeping the sweet harmony and balance in their life. The hustle and bustle of life can be compared to the thief in the bible. "The thief comes only to steal and kill and destroy; I came that they may have life and have it abundantly" (John 10:10 ESV). God desires that you have a life full of happiness and contentment.

As with any institution, it is crucial to carve out time for what's important or really matters, otherwise you risk the possibility of suffering immensely. Couples must be intentional about making time for each other, especially as daily life pulls at you individually, perhaps as parents, employees, and leaders within your community or an organization.

My husband would often say "whatever it took to get my wife, (flowers, dinners, romantic gestures, flirting, long night talks on the phone, or sun set strolls holding hands) I have to do that and then some to keep her. Safeguarding your time together is a key, but what you do with that time is of equal importance. Making time for fun and interesting things is a safeguard against the mundane and predictable boredom of life. Dullness can easily settle into a couple's routine.

For us it may be date night once a week, it may be more or less frequent for other couples, however "date night" is imperative to keeping the romance and excitement going in your relationship. Establishing that your time with each other is a priority, and is to be honored before board meeting, children, sports events, and other commitments. Fun time together is vital to the survival of a healthy and happy couple. After all, when your careers take a turn in another direction, the children are grown and leave the nest, or life happens, what will you have left?

Bringing more things to the table besides Netflix, or every Friday at the same restaurant, make your time together beautiful and vibrant. Laughing together a lot and often, celebrating more than Valentine's day, anniversaries and birthdays is important.

My husband and I have been blessed. As a couple we have been afforded opportunities that many couples have not. We've traveled throughout the entire North American continent, Mexico, Canada and 37 out of the 50 states and vacationed in several Caribbean island and cruised. Along these journeys we've met fascinating people and had incredibly exciting times. But some of the most amazing adventures we shared together have been just sitting at local beaches, each of us with our own book, basking in the sun together splitting a bag of chips. Making cherished memories together doesn't always have to entail spending enormous amounts of money or even going to exotic places. We've managed to have a wonderful time having an indoor picnic, eating sandwiches together on a blanket in the living room, no TV, social media, or children. We would just go to the basketball court and play horse, challenge each other to see who could answer the most questions correctly as we watched the TV show Jeopardy or answer the word puzzles on "Wheel of Fortune". Not only is my husband funny but he has a competitive streak. At times in our marriage money has been low and stresses high. This is the perfect storm brewing to counter act your ability to enjoy each other's company.

I will never forget our 16ᵗʰ wedding anniversary. Financially we were struggling and a sweet family member decided to bless us with a weekend hotel stay about 60 miles from our home, situated on the ocean along with a two part gift card valued at $50.00 ($25 allocated to the movies / $25 to Applebee's Restaurant). She made all the arrangements and provided the childcare, therefore saying no was not an option. We accepted graciously, however, inside each of us was unexcited because we realized that we didn't have money to put gas in the car or provide for our other weekend meals. We ventured off for the weekend, trusting and praying that God would provide. Apprehensively we entered Applebee's and purchased a 2 for $20 meal, each drank water and left what remained on the gift card with some change for the tip. Following dinner, we proceeded to the movie and a cozy night stay. The next day, thankfully with hotel breakfast included, we embarked around town looking for free fun things to do, and on our actual anniversary day after skipping lunch, we sat in McDonald's with items from the dollar menu for dinner. I will never forget the look on my husband's face as we ate. I could sense that he was wounded inside, in hopes that after all these years of marriage, we would be in a better place, but with a smile on my face I begin to make jokes about the chicken sandwich tasting like the best "Mickey D's" had ever prepared. I remember saying "how sweet of them to celebrate us in this way, by placing extra lettuce on my sandwich in recognition of our sweet 16" and making mention that we had never been to a McDonalds near the water. The ocean breeze added a little additional savor making the food taste more distinctive! He chimed in with comments about his meal and the two of us laughed and laughed until he almost spit his dollar drink out. Although the memory of our financial woe is even hard to recount today, I am reminded of how important fun and laughter are to a relationship no matter how difficult your circumstance. Out of all the 30 anniversary's we have shared, that remains the most special. It's not memorable because I remember that money was low, it's magical because I realized how rich we actually were! We were determined to have fun at dinner time and always! The laughter was then and remains the sofrito to our marriage.

Laughter and fun are an amazing gift from God. It helps you cope with sadness and everyday life. Have you ever felt mad and then someone said something to make you laugh? Even though you were upset the laughter made your heart feel better. "I will bless the LORD at all times: his praise shall continually be in my mouth" (Psalms 34:1 KJV). Certainly in life, heartache will come and you may not feel like being entertained let alone entertaining, you may want to retire off into a secluded room and bury yourself under a blanket, and that is your choice, but I'd like to encourage you with the words of Charlie Chaplin, "A day without laughter is a day wasted".

As a couple, build each other up and surround yourself with people and things that bring the best out in you. Amuse each other and steer clear of monotony, the bible declares that "A joyful heart makes a cheerful face, but with a heartache comes depression" (Proverbs 15:13 GWT). Sorrow is an enemy to joy and fun, therefore remember,

> surround yourself with people and things that bring the best out in you

when troubled times come don't remain defeated. Don't allow it to steal away your fun and peace. Don't keep the blanket over your head too long, rise, embrace each other, and have fun.

I previously stated that sofrito can be store bought but it's no match for the "real thing". Preparation of the authentic condiment may be frustrating, take much more time and effort. In fact, it can be quite stressful if you've never attempted to create it before. However, with practice every batch of the recipe formulated will become easier and easier. Such is the same if fun has not been part of your daily routine. It may seem challenging at first, and perhaps you've been in the relationship for a while and venturing out into the fun realm may feel exasperating. Be assured, with baby steps in a forward direction and a commitment to genuinely appreciating leisure time together those moments will become meaningful and pleasant. Having fun can be thrilling, soothing, and rejuvenating, it can be exactly what the good chef ordered!

"I know it is wet and the sun is not sunny, but we can have lots of good fun that is funny" Dr. Seuss

Simmer (Fun)

1. List four fun places that you would like to visit as a couple within the next twelve months.

2. Upon arriving at those fun locations, what do you anticipate you will do there?

3. What are some free and fun things you can incorporate into your lives each week?

Prayer

Lord, you came that we may have life and that life more abundantly. As we organize our residence, schedules, and daily functions, help us to be mindful to incorporate fun, laughter and love into our life. Illuminate your peace so that we not only strive to exist, but we thrive joyfully in this existence. Point out areas that need improvement then stir up creativity and joy to occupy that space. In Jesus name, Amen.

INGREDIENT 7
FINANCE
No Leftovers

Recipe: Finance French Toast

Ingredients:

A bundle of budget

A serving of saving

1lb of prayer

8 cups wisdom

Directions:

Pour wisdom into the bundle of budget. Smother with prayer, allow to rise 2 hours. Bake for 10 minutes at 425 and then 20 minutes at 350. Serve alongside the serving of saving.

*"Every day is a bank account, and time is our currency.
No one is rich, no one is poor, we've got 24 hours each".*
Christopher Rice

Certainly, whether eating out or doing the groceries for the home, someone has to pay the bill. There is nothing worse than going out to eat and having to pay for a meal that didn't quite hit the mark. When your favorite dish is not prepared to your satisfaction the idea of having to pay for it is less than stunning. On the contrary, you never feel gloomy about paying when you've gotten your money's worth; Everything about the meal was perfect, proper portions, taste is divine, no doggie bag needed, your belly is full and no leftovers.

Having made investments and not received a return, or pouring your blood, sweat and tears into a project just for it to flop is heartbreaking. When you invest in your marriage you want to see the fruits of your labor. Unfortunately, that is not always the case. Regardless of how much you plant and sow, if the finances are in a shamble regrettably almost every other area of your life will follow. I've heard it said many times of money and marriage, "when the money is funny everything is funny". Finances can be tricky, whether in lack or overflow, surplus or shortfall, without the willingness of both parties to agree on the way they view and discuss basic money principals within their marriage, undoubtably severe issues will arise.

Initially, every couple is on the same page. Many will stand in the presence of witnesses and declare the words "for richer or poorer" in "good times and bad", however, often spouses can't survive either the richer or poorer due to weak money management skills.

Couples disagree over who will handle the money, who will pay the bills, should they undergo a joint or separate account, do we split everything 50/50? Should the "bread winner" assume all the financial responsibility? Some spouses stick to their own way of managing their money, while others may lie, cheat, and overspend. All of these inadequate decisions cause a breach in trust; inevitably wearing away at the very fiber of the relationship. How can we help newlyweds or even seasons married people prevent these controversial views from invading your marriage?

Although this book's primary focus is the overall relationship and not solely on finances, I'd like to offer three simple suggestions, if you find your marriage in financial distress. Rule #1, remain hopeful with God in the center, now is not the time to question can we repair our relationship if financial disaster has taken hold. You absolutely can not only repair but renew! "What do you mean, 'If I can'?" Jesus stated, "Anything is possible if a person believes" (Mark 9:23 NLT). Don't allow financial mishaps to determine your destiny. Avoid thoughts of despair which ultimately produce destruction in a relationship. In fact, the proper attitude toward money management can actually be a rewarding way to bond with your loved one. Remaining optimistic and patient as you learn to get better through the process. "Not that I speak from want, for I have learned to be content in whatever circumstances I am. I know how to get along with humble means, and I also know how-to live-in prosperity; in any and every circumstance I have learned the secret of being filled and going hungry, both of having abundance and suffering need. I can do all things through Him who strengthens me" (Philippians 4:11-13 NASB). Eventually as you work with God and each other good habits and financial growth will be produced.

Planning ahead would be a good rule #2. Ideally, the best way to approach financial discussion would be prior to marriage, after all if preparation releases prosperity then procrastination would surely release poverty "The plans of the diligent lead to profit as surely as haste leads to poverty" (Proverbs 21:5 NIV). Therefore, the noblest suggestion would be to carefully plan out the intricate details of money before walking down the aisle. Nevertheless, "life happens", careers changes, employment options become few, and secure financial planning may nose-dive. Often times the best intended plans and groundwork fails. Tragic situations unquestionably necessitate that a couple go back to the drawing board or simply agree to disagree. If deep discussions of money matters are avoided prior to the nuptials, committing to working through the process on the road to better, with an understanding heart is always appropriate.

"Which of you, desiring to build a tower, does not first sit down and count the costs, whether he had enough to complete it?" (Luke 14:28 ESV). Too often, couples put off planning until they are so deeply in debt that it seems impossible to get out. That's not planning, it's reacting. Having a good understanding of money can save you loads of headaches and an abundance of time and energy. Dave Ramsey once said, "You must gain control over your money or the lack of it will forever control you." From the onset, money topics should be on top of the list.

It is unlikely for a couple to have their finances under control if they neglect the basic understanding of good record keeping. Couples need to educate themselves, in addition to discovering each other's financial practices. It's imperative to identify, if she is a spender or saver, inquire if he is frugal or generous. Awareness of spending habits and credit scores can only enhance the health and wealth within a relationship. The bible says, "He that hath no rule over his own spirit is like a city that is broken down, and without walls" (Proverbs 25:28 KJV). It's vital to know if your future spouse has control over their money or their money has control over them. Healthy financial boundaries are essential.

If the two of you can't agree on how money should be managed, then it will be exceedingly difficult to walk together into a prosperous future "Can two people walk together without agreeing on the direction?" (Amos 3:3 NLT). The one who is stronger, wiser, and disciplined in the financial area should assume the role of record keeper. The institution of two bookkeeper's usually induces misfortune. After the proper plan has been initiated and written down with firm goals established, including a balanced budget, commit to reviewing these goals frequently.

Finally, rule #3 sticking to the plan that you have laid out before you as a couple is key. If you work the plan, the plan will work. Money is a help when used correctly. "For wisdom *is* a defense, *and* money *is* a defense: but the excellency of knowledge *is, that* wisdom giveth life to them that have it" (Ecclesiastes 7:12 KJV). Lack of money isn't always the problem within a marriage, often times it just boils down to the fact that the individuals are not remaining true to the plan. If you approach your finances with the philosophy "The more you make the more you spend" regardless of the plan, you are guaranteed to create heap of problems between a husband and wife. Surplus without a plan is not a blessing. Stay within budget, don't borrow more than you can pay, talk about money often and remaining transparent with your thoughts concerning the plan are all crucial to a financial free marriage. "The rich rule over the poor, and the borrower is servant to the lender" (Proverbs 22:7 KJV). Discussing the route in which you plan to travel and not deviating from the path no matter how much revenue is funneling through your account is a sure way to arrive safely at the door of your goals and dreams.

With three decades under our belt, we certainly have had our share of financial victory and defeat. On many occasions, we often choose to deviate from the plan and then there were times when the plan chose to change on us. Either way, over the years we had our fair share of adjusting. The year I graduated college was also the same year we got married. We had counted the cost for our wedding and planned for an extravagant event with 16 in the wedding party and 200 guests invited. We were looking forward to the beautiful summer day. However, we were hit with unexpected end of year college bills and fees that consumed a portion of our wedding budget. It was a difficult time to navigate through. For most, the planning of a wedding our size is quite stressful. Compiling that with wanting to graduate from college on time, with the weight of knowing you cannot walk across the stage until all financial obligations have been met, we faced a gigantic dilemma. Determined to succeed at both and unable to do it alone, we were compelled to turn to family for assistance. Once the college financial office was in receipt of all their funds and financial responsibilities were met for wedding commitment, we had no leftovers. The wonderful part of this story is that I graduated with honors as scheduled and our wedding was everything we dreamed. Unfortunately, within the few short months of planning for each huge life changing event some family relationships suffered injury along the way. As a young couple we were emotionally rocked by life's big events and the astronomical amount of money that comes with them. With everything coming our way, many feelings were hurt in the process, ours included.

> Never underestimate the power of people's willingness to help you

I share this story in hopes that you will understand that no matter what you may be facing financially as you read through these pages know that you are going to make it. Never underestimate the power of people's willingness to help you and most importantly, at the end of the day it's only money. Money is like hair. It grows back, don't let it ruin you or cause damage to your relationship with your spouse or others.

"Don't save what is left after spending; spend what is left after saving" Warren Buffett

Simmer (Finance)

1. Can you pinpoint areas in your finances that need improvement?

2. What steps are you taking toward achieving financial security within your marriage?

3. Write down three financial goals, that you will accomplish within the next twelve months?

Prayer

Faithful Father, God of more than enough, every good and perfect gift comes from above, money is our defense and gift from you, help us to be good and faithful stewards over our finances. We trust you to help us develop wisdom and make solid informed decision concerning money. Let us work together to identity weak areas within our finances and adjust quickly to correct any intolerable behaviors. Thank you in advance for the increase and honor our obedience to your word as it relates to financial gains. In Jesus name, Amen.

DESSERT ANYONE?

Dessert after dinner, has always been my favorite! I remember being a child and living for dessert after our meals. Whether it was one chocolate chip cookie, a baked cinnamon apple or fruit cocktail, it always seemed to be the most enjoyable time of day. Often times I had to fight my way through dinner. It was a real struggle to eat what I didn't like, possibly the sweet peas or brussels sprouts, but the rule in our house was you must eat all your food and leave a clean plate before you could indulge in dessert. Such is the same for couples. You may have to fight your way through all the agony of twists, dislikes, ups and downs in the relationship. Perhaps your struggle is finances, lack of fun and

> Clean the plate, meaning little by little you will have to eat away at whatever is attempting to eat away at your marriage.

sex or failed communication. I can only encourage you that after the pushing and pressing through mealtime a sweet treat is on the other side. Don't give up, remain in the fight.

Clean the plate, meaning little by little you will have to eat away at whatever is attempting to eat away at your marriage. Don't leave any unturned stone, give your marriage your all, it's worth it.

My grandmother knew that by eating all the "good stuff" like the vegetables even if perhaps I despised them, I would grow up to be big and strong. In marriage everything isn't always going to taste good, but it is good for you. Overcoming the tough things will make your relationship big and strong. Every choice is a potential habit that affects your lifestyle.

Many nights I would be the last person at the table because we were not allowed to get up until everything was gone. Being left alone, I would imagine that the spinach was actually the dessert only to enable me to digest it. In an effort to cheer myself on, I would choose to change my mind set in order to view my ill situation as manageable. My viewpoint was from a childish perspective because the reality was it wasn't that bad at all. "And we know that all things work together for good to them that love God, to them who are the called according to *his* purpose" (Roman 8:28 KJV).

Sometimes you may feel left as though you are the only one at the table and it may be lonely, but you're never alone. In that time alone at the table I grew, I learned strategies of eating what I hated first, or eating it fast. As the plate was places in front of me, I would quickly assess if there were some of my non favorites on it and begin to think about what I would do. Those rough nights trying to swallow what I loathed seemed unbearable, but the time and space apart from the family only proved that my grandmother knew what was best for me. I hung in there and got my reward in the form of dessert. When unbearable times hit your relationship and your each trying to navigate through a detested situation, I would like to cheer you on to change your view point, give each other space to grow, work on personal strategies, develop individual passions and hobbies, and you too will become strong enough to embrace the unlovable parts of your spouse. Conceivably the good chef knows what's best for you.

No matter how full I felt, I always saved room for dessert. Someway, somehow, I would inflate my stomach or push that food down into the digestive tract. It was as if I was working through what seemed impossible. That was because I wanted to enjoy the sweet treat. Despite how uncomfortable I felt, if dessert was on my mind, dessert was what I would have. Even if Nana said "your eyes are bigger than your stomach" I couldn't resist her something scrumptious.

If your relationship needs healing, you may feel like you can't handle anymore, fed up and completely full. I can only encourage you to inflate your mind, expand your willingness to work through what seems impossible, so that you too can make room for the sweet course that awaits you. The most difficult circumstance can eventually give way to delight and gratification. It is a push at times, physically and mentally exhausting, and all roads are leading up hill, but eventually the night will give way to the light. Remain on the road together in it for the long haul. After all it's amazing to witness God exceed what we believe to be possible. "Now to him who is able to do immeasurably more than all we ask or imagine, according to his power that is at work within us" (Ephesians 3:20 NIV).

I can recall a time when I was in high school and I ran track. During my junior year for some unseen reason, I began to faint during my races. Medical attention was necessary. It was a very scary time. Although I felt physically fit, my body was telling me something else. The doctor ordered a sleep study and an EEG test which required me to stay up for 18-24 hours. In an effort to break night I enlisted the help of my husband, (boyfriend at the time) and two of our close friends. Their job was to help me to not fall asleep. We played cards, board games for hours and as our eyes grew weary, we decided to move our entertaining outdoors on a very cold New England night to have wheel barrel races and other competitive games in hopes that the physical activity and brisk air would pass the time. As the morning drew near and the sun began to rise, we opted for a long walk up a hill to the local gas station for snacks. Needless to say, that hill became my breaking point, I was in an incredibly low place. All of that physical activity had overwhelmed me. I could feel my soul wanting to cave under the pressure. My mind, after being deprived sleep, was beginning to play tricks on me. My future husband and friends were my dessert.

They made it clear that we would finish out that rough night together. They were in it with me for the long haul. I had to remind myself that I was strong and with nothing left, their moral support was like a cherry on top of my ice cream.

I am fully aware that it is not always easy trying to maintain a physically, emotionally, and spiritually healthy relationship at all times. In every relationship you will hit a hill or drop into a valley. Perhaps, you may currently find yourself at a low point in life or in your relationship, always remain alert to what dessert God will send in the desert.

The road to recovery mentally and physically can be tough, and at times you may not have the moral support of your spouse, but you must remind yourself that you too are strong enough to finish this race, together you can make it! "That is why, for Christ's sake, I delight in weaknesses, in insults, in hardships, in persecutions, in difficulties. For when I am weak, then I am strong" (II Corinthians 12:10 NIV). In track and marriage there is a prize at the finish line. Hang in there and you two will enjoy the dessert of life unruffled. We have been fortunate to have survived the many of life's twist and turns, up hills and down valleys. It is only because of the grace and mercy of the Lord and our desire to enjoy the dessert together, we have succeeded. We have witnessed over the years, on many occasions, the night give way to light and dessert after dinner has remained our favorite. We are determined to leave nothing left on the plate, whatever it takes, we will live full and die empty.

"Do not be anxious about anything, but in every situation, by prayer and petition, with thanksgiving, present your requests to God" (Philippians 4:6 NIV)

LATE NIGHT SNACK?

This is just a little something extra to think about. Have you ever considered divorce? I mean really considered the whole outcome. The complete unadulterated finale that no one seems to talk about, especially when children are involved.

The reality is one out of two marriages in America will end in the courtroom. These shocking statistics are staggering. Although there are many reasons and causes behind it that are difficult to understand, the impacts are usually catastrophic, leaving most people unprepared for the future fallout.

I speak of this to give you cold hard facts not to convince you to stay, just offering something for you to chew on or mull over if perhaps after reading this book you're still on the fence.

Statistics show that over one million children suffer the decision made by their parents to end a relationship. It has physical, emotional, and financial effects on children. Here are just a few statistics to consider!

Children whose parents have terminated their marriage, become the victims of abuse. They are also prone to more health, behavioral, and emotional problems that ultimately lead to drug abuse and even suicide. The academic performances of such children are poor. Such children are three times more likely to have emotional or behavioral problems than they will have if their biological parents stay together.

When parents end their marriage, there is dramatic change in children's attitude towards sexual behavior. Children's approval of premarital sex and cohabitation and divorce rises dramatically, while their endorsement of marriage and childbearing is reduced.

Children of divorced parents move away from their families of origin more than children of intact marriages. To a large degree, the marital instability of one generation is passed on to the next. This lowered quality of marriage for children of divorced couples is a big matter of concern.

Divorce gives birth to higher levels of jealousy, moodiness, infidelity, conflicts over money, and excessive drinking and drug use amongst children.

Children in the age groups of 8-11 feel a lot of anger and powerlessness and tend to favor and care for one parent over the other. For children in the age groups of 12-18, the grief becomes more intense and they tend to focus more on the moral issues causing them to judge their parents and become more fearful for the relationships they will have in the future.

BIBLICAL BUFFET

(recipes for strength, one for each day of the week)

"Above all, love each other deeply, because love covers over a multitude of sins." (I Peter 4:8 NIV)

"Husbands love your wives and be not bitter against them." (Col 3:19 KJV)

"Let all *that* you *do* be done with love." (I Cor 16:14 ESV)

"Beloved, let us love one another: for love is of God; and everyone that loveth is born of God, and knoweth God." (I John 4:7 KJV)

"Beloved, if God so loved us, we ought also to love one another." (I John 4:11 KJV)

"My little children, let us not love in word or in tongue, but indeed and in truth." (I John 3:18 NKJV)

"Wives submit yourselves unto your own husbands, as unto the Lord. For the husband is the head of the wife, even as Christ is the head of the church: and he is the savior of the body. Therefore, as the church is subject unto Christ, so let the wives be to their own husbands in everything. Husbands, love your wives, even as Christ also loved the church, and gave himself for it." (Eph 5:22-25 KJV)

Southern Style Collard Greens Recipe

2 cups chicken stock

Smoked turkey leg

1 onion, diced

1 tablespoon seasoned salt

1 cup vinegar

1 tablespoon crushed red peppers

4-6 bunches of clean-cut collard greens

In a pan place chicken stock, turkey leg, onion, seasoned salt, vinegar, and crushed red pepper. Bring to a boil. Add cut collard greens. Bring back to a boil and then reduce to lowest setting to simmer for an hour.

Puerto Rican Style Rice and Beans Recipe

1 tablespoon Olive Oil

2 heaping tablespoons Sofrito (homemade preferred)

1 packet Goya Sazon Con Culantro y Achiote

½ teaspoon each Onion powder and Garlic powder

8 ounce can Goya Tomato Sauce

1 cube Knorr Caldo Con Sabor de Pollo (Chicken Bouilon)

1 can Gandules (Pigeon Peas)

Olives (to taste)

1 cup Rice (long grain)

1 ½ cup Water

Recaito leaves

Rinse rice and set aside. Heat your caldero (that special Latino pot) to medium heat and add olive oil and Sofrito. Stir constantly for about 3-4 minutes.

Stir in the Sazon, garlic and onion powder along with tomato sauce and chicken bouillon.

Add in the Gandules pigeon peas and olives (to taste) bring to slight boil, then stir in rice. Add water and lay the recaito leave on top, cover with a tight lid, reduce heat, and cook for about 20-25 minutes.

Allow the rice to absorb all the visible liquid. Once most of the liquid has evaporated, stir the rice into a pyramid, cover once again.

Finally, allow the steam to finish the job. Rice is done when all the liquid is absorbed, and the grains are dry and fluffy.

I am praying for you!

I am praying for you. It is my prayer that everyone who picked up a copy of this book has received some blessing, a nugget, or a word of encouragement to push forward.

If you are not married or are preparing to be married, may the ingredients within these pages speak life and give you some guidance of how to create a healthy relationship with your soon to be spouse.

I'd love to hear from you, follow me at the following and let me know what your favorite chapter was by making mention of it referencing social media handles for example #perseverance, or #Iburntthemeal

On Facebook:
Denisha Sanchez
https://www.facebook.com/denisha.sanchez.121

Instagram:
denishasanchez1

Website:
denishasanchez.com

CPSIA information can be obtained
at www.ICGtesting.com
Printed in the USA
LVHW022239121120
671376LV00009B/532